# A Framework for Measuring Organizational Intangible Assets

SUDHIR WARIER

# DEDICATION

To the Supreme Being ......

# CONTENTS

# PREFACE

Intellectual Capital remains the most unexploited resource within an organization. Knowledge continues to be seen as a static organizational asset. This is especially true for organizations in the Indian subcontinent. The tremendous growth in the different fields of management and research contributions in the last decade have not helped in addressing all the limitations in measurement models. The framework presented in this book builds on the advantages and the robustness of the Balanced Score Card while doing away with some of its primary limitations, namely rigidity, traditional financial measures, lack of employee perspective etc. The deployment of Intellectual Capital measurement, Economic Value Added and Human Resource Accounting techniques within the modified six dimensional framework is unique and provides a more holistic measurement framework.

The framework presented in this book is more than just a collection of measures. It is imperative that all measures should be allied through a causative chain that terminates with a linkage to monetary performance. The effectiveness of the strategic direction of an organization should be monitored continually to get a feedback on its framework. The organization should effect single measure changes and check its effects till it manages to fine-tune all the metrics in the framework. This is a continual process wherein the cause-and-effect relationships are modified cyclically.

*Sudhir Warier*

SUDHIR WARIER

# LIST OF TABLES

**Page is Intentionally Blank**

# LIST OF FIGURES

**Page is Intentionally Blank**

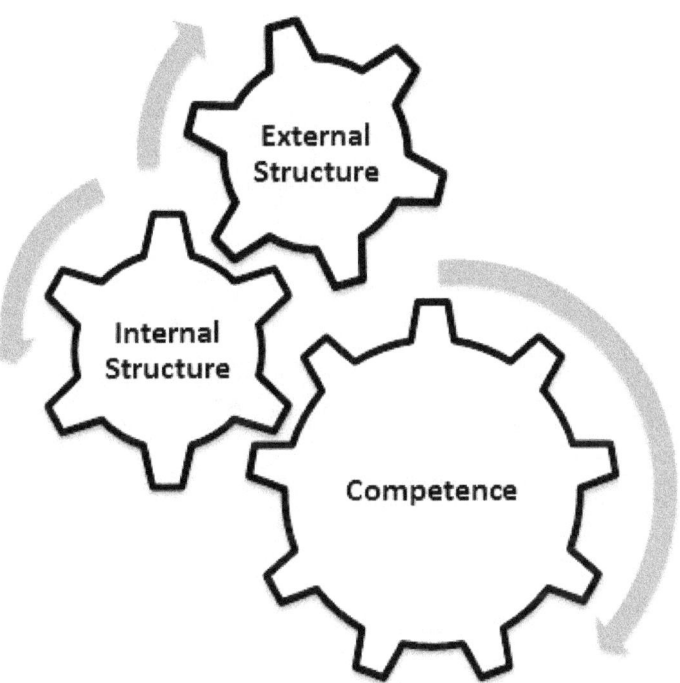

*"Knowledge has no value until it is put into action"*
*Sudhir Warier*

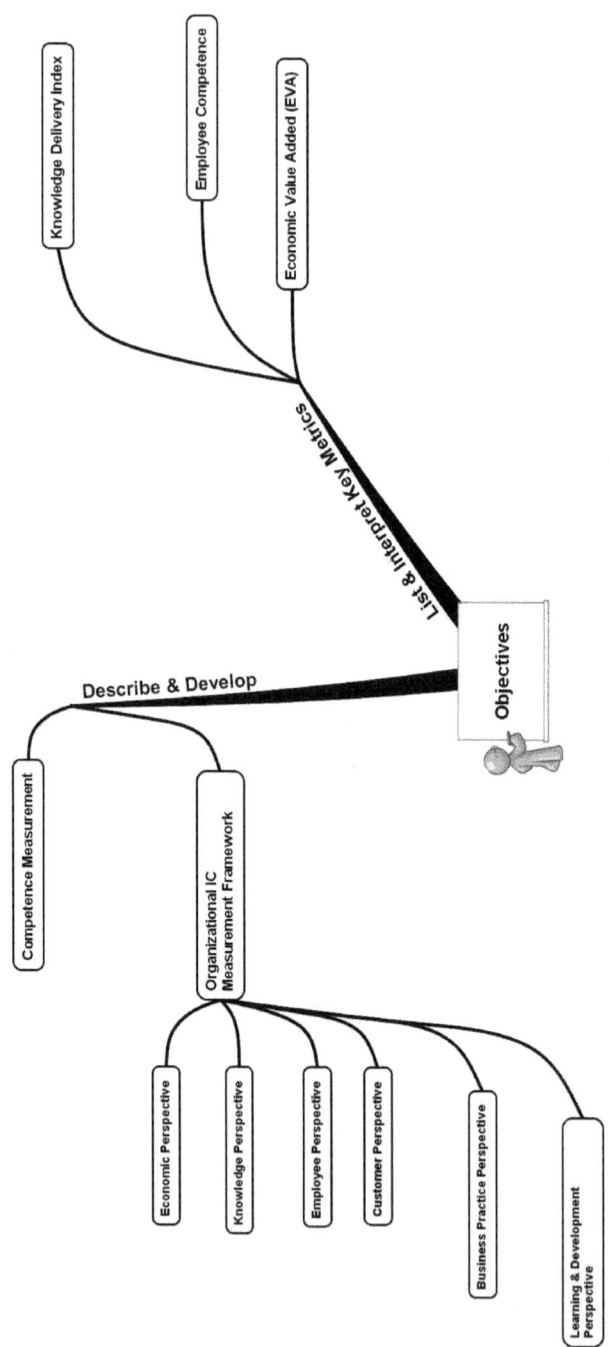

# 1 INTANGIBLE ASSETS

## Introduction

Accurate measurement enables an organization to identify the initiatives that provide the maximum return-on-investment (ROI). The organization can subsequently focus its efforts on these initiatives while still continuing to work on areas likely to yield results in the short, medium and long term. Organizations tend to believe they are performing well; measurement confirms or denies such beliefs.

One of the major hindrances in the deployment of Competency (Competence) Management systems is the lack of objective measures for gauging the value of the human capital and the effectiveness of the deployed system itself. It may be noted that organizations will not benefit by simply developing metrics for measuring competence. A holistic framework that measures the intellectual capital (IC) or Knowledge Capital and IC flows within an organization is required.

This chapter provides a measurement framework, with an emphasis on the measurement of intangible assets, based on the Balanced Scorecard along with metrics to employee competence.

SUDHIR WARIER

## Organizational Intellectual Capital

Knowledge Capital is the value that a customer assigns to an organization in addition to the value of its physical assets . It is the surplus value in excess of the traditional value. The employees are the bearers of the Knowledge Capital and act as repositories of organizational knowledge and culture. They are shareholders of the most important asset a firm owns. However these intangible aspects can never be reflected in the traditional accounting systems. The current methodologies use a bottom up method of evaluating the knowledge assets of an organization. The total Knowledge Capital is calculated by summing up the value of patents, products and services including software and trained manpower. This method does not reflect the true value of knowledge which requires a top-down approach. This approach calls for a valuation of the output before the valuation the input and is reflected in the capacity of an organization to receive revenue from customers willing to pay a premium for the knowledge, in addition to the capital goods, services and manufacturing capabilities offered. The enterprise Knowledge Capital is of no worth until the customer recognizes the value of knowledge offered by the organization. The important aspect, which needs to be realized, is that is that there is a premium on Knowledge Capital that should be added to the financial equity value. The final value would then reflect the value perceived by the stock market. According to Paul Strassman a leading proponent of this concept, the sum of knowledge capital of an organization and the shareholder book equity would result in a value that is a close approximation of the stock market evaluation of the organization.

# 2 MEASURING ORGANIZATIONAL INTANGIBLE ASSETS

The value of the intellectual capital of any organization and the efficiency and performance its management systems cannot be measured by the conventional tools and techniques in existence. There is no difference between monetary measures and other measures. Both are uncertain and are dependent on the observer. There exist no "objective" measures. Knowledge flows and intangible assets are essentially non- monetary. Most organizations measure at least some of their intangible assets and they use non-monetary indicators particularly for measuring operational efficiency. Manufacturing companies have for instance measure their output in "output per hour", hospitals and hotels measure bed utilization, and schools measure student's performance in terms of marks. Customer relations, such as satisfaction levels and competence related measures; such as employee satisfaction and retention are still not monitored on a regular basis by most organizations. The problem does not lie in designing systems for intangible measurements but lies in the interpretation of the results of these systems. Customer surveys, for instance, when used systematically results in an abundance of data which managers find difficult to correlate with changes in business performance. The following were some of the commonly used techniques in measuring the value of intangible assets:

1. **Relative Value** - Bob Buckman (Buckman Laboratories) and Leif Edvinsson (Skandia Insurance) are proponents of this approach, in which progress, not a quantitative target, is the ultimate goal. *Example:* have 80% of employees involved with the customer in some meaningful way.

2. **Balanced Scorecard (BSC)** - Supplements traditional financial measures with three additional perspectives -- customers, internal business processes, and learning/growth.

3. **Competency Models** - By observing and classifying the behaviours of "successful" employees ("competency models") and calculating the market value of their output, it's possible to assign a rupee value to the intellectual capital they create and use in their work.

4. **Subsystem Performance** – It is easier to quantify success or progress in area within the organization. *For example* an R&D organization may be able to measure an increase in royalty revenues through effective management of its intellectual property (patents).

5. **Benchmarking** – This involves identifying companies that are recognized leaders in leveraging their intellectual assets, determining how well they score on relevant criteria, and then comparing own performance against that of the leaders. *Example* of a relevant criterion: Identification of knowledge gaps and defining processes to eliminate the gaps.

6. **Business Worth** - This approach centers estimating the monetary value of crucial organizational information and/or knowledge through forecasting techniques. For example – Effect on organizational profitability of the amount of crucial information/knowledge generated by the organization is doubled.

7. **Business Process Auditing** – The involves measuring the value addition of information and knowledge for key organizational processes - accounting, production, marketing, or ordering.

8. **Knowledge Bank** - This involves a modification of generally accepted accounting principles – Capital spending is considered as an asset while a portion of

6

salaries is treated as an asset (based on the premise that it creates future cash flows).

9. **Brand Equity Valuation** – This involves the use of a methodology that measures the economic impact of a brand (or other intangible asset) on such things as pricing power, distribution reach, ability to launch new products.

10. **Calculated Intangible Value** – This involves comparison of the organizations Return on Assets (ROA) with the industry ROA to obtain a measure of the organizational IC value.

11. **Microlending** – Institutions that support micro lending substitute intangible "collateral" (peer group support, training, and the personal qualities of entrepreneurs) for tangible assets.

According to Luthy (1998) and Williams (2000) all methods can be divided into four main groups:

a. **Direct Intellectual Capital Methods (DICM)** – These methods work on the principle of estimating the monetary value of intangible assets by identifying and evaluating its various components.

b. **Market Capitalization Methods (MCM)** – These methods calculate the difference between the market capitalization of an organization and its stockholder's. This difference represents the value of its intellectual capital.

c. **Return on Assets Methods (ROA)** – These methods estimate the value of an organizations intellectual capital by computing the average earnings (pre-tax) of the enterprise and divide them by the average tangible assets. The resultant ROA can be compared across industries. The difference multiplied by the organizations average tangible assets provides the average annual earnings from intangibles. The earnings divided by the weighted average cost of capital provides the value of Intangible assets.

d. **Scorecard Methods (SC)** – A scorecard lists the components of intangible assets along with the relevant indicators and indices

The table 1 lists some of the commonly employed methods for organizational intangible assets valuation/;

Table 1 – Intangible Assets Valuation Methods (Jolanta Jurczak, 2008)

| S.N | Methodology | Inventor | Brief Description |
|-----|-------------|----------|-------------------|
| 1 | Accounting for the Future (AFTF) | Nash (1998) | A system of projected discounted cash flows |
| 2 | Balanced Score Card | Kaplan & Norton (1996) | Organizational performance measurement based on indicators based on four perspectives – Financial, Customer Internal Process Learning |
| 3 | Calculated Intangible Value | Stewart (1997) Luthy (1998) | Proportion of organizational revenue attributed to intangible assets |
| 4 | Citation Weighted Patents | Bontis (1996) | Measure based on the impact of R&D efforts - Number of patents, Cost of patents to sales turnover |
| 5 | Competency Index | Sudhir Warier (2014) | Measure individual competency development and flows |
| 6 | Competency Quotient | Sudhir Warier (2011) | Evaluate individual competencies |
| 7 | Organizational Value (Knowledge Quotient) Measurement (OKQ) | Sudhir Warier (2005) | Evaluate, measure organizational value creation based on six perspectives |

| | Framework | | |
|---|---|---|---|
| 8 | Economic Value Added (EVA) | Stewart (1997) | Residual value in excess of all organizational expenses |
| 9 | Human Capital Intelligence | Fitz-Enz (1994) | Benchmarking of human capital indicators |
| 10 | Human Resource Costing & Accounting (HRCA) | Johansson (1997) | Calculate impact of HR related costs |
| 11 | Intangible Asset Monitor | Sveiby (1997) | Measure four aspects of value creation from intangible assets - Growth, Renewal, Utilization, Efficiency, Risk reduction/ stability |
| 12 | Intellectual Asset Valuation | Sullivan (2000) | Methodology for assessing the value of Intellectual Property. |
| 13 | Intellectual Capital Navigator and Intellectual Capital Index (IC Index™) | Roos & Others (1997) | Conception diagram illustrating the usage of organizations intellectual capital |
| 14 | Investor Assigned Market Value (IAMV™) | Standfield (1998) | Market value of organizations shares divided by Tangible Capital+(Realized Intellectual Capital + Intellectual Capital Erosion+ Sustainable Competitive |

| | | | Advantage |
|---|---|---|---|
| 15 | Knowledge Capital Earnings | Lev (1999) | Portion of normalized earnings over and above expected earnings attributable to book asset |
| 16 | Market-to- Book Value | Stewart (1997) Luthy (1998) | Difference between the organizations share value and book value |
| 17 | Skandia Navigator™ | Edvinsson & Malone (1997) | Measurement of intellectual capital through analysis of 164 metric measures |
| 18 | Technology Broker | Brooking (1996) | Valuation based on Market Assets, Human-centred Assets, Intellectual Property Assets and Infrastructure Assets |
| 19 | The Value Explorer™ | Andriessen & Tiessen (2000) | Methodology designed by KMPG for calculating and allocating value to 5 types of intangibles: Assets and endowments, Skills & tacit knowledge, Collective values and norms, Technology and explicit knowledge, Primary and management processes |

| 20 | Tobin's q S | Stewart (1997) | Ratio of the market value of the organizations shares to the replacement cost of its assets |
|---|---|---|---|
| 21 | Total Value Creation (TVC™) | Anderson & McLean (2000) | Evaluate impact of events on planned activities based on discounted projected cash-flow |
| 22 | Value Added Intellectual Coefficient (VAIC™) | Pulic (1997) | Measure value creation of intellectual assets |
| 23 | Value Chain Scoreboard™ | Lev (2002) | Matrix of non-financial indicators based on development cycles -Discovery, Learning, Implementation, Commercialization |
| 24 | Value Creation Index | Ittner & Others (2000) | Derive drivers of value creation |

# 3 THE MEASUREMENT FRAMEWORK – ORGANIZATIONAL KNOWLEDGE QUOTIENT (OKQ)

Competence represents the intellectual or knowledge capital of an enterprise. Competence differentiates an enterprise from its competition and provides value to the brand. It is therefore appropriate that competence is measured as a part of the overall intellectual capital of an organization. This would provide a true measure of its value and contribution to the EVA. An attempt to measure competence on its own would not be accurate and undervalue its importance in creating long term value for the organization. The framework presented here is based on the BSC and validated through empirical research. However this model differs in many key areas and provides flexibility as compared to the BSC. In a BSC the perspectives drive the identification of strategic organizational initiatives. This is limiting, because most ares will be multi perspective and have simultaneous impact on multiple dimensions of organizational intangible assets (Bontis, Dragonetti, Jacobsen & Roos, 1999).

The OKQ framework, illustrated in the figure 1, organizes its measurement system across six key contexts.

1. Economic Context
2. Knowledge Context
3. Employee (Knowledge Worker) Context
4. Customer Context

5. Business Practice Context
   a. Business Processes
   b. Generic Processes
   c. Knowledge Processes
      i. *Knowledge Creation Process*
      ii. *Knowledge Processing Process*
      iii. *Knowledge Storage & Renewal Process*
      iv. *Knowledge Sharing Process*
6. Learning & Development Context

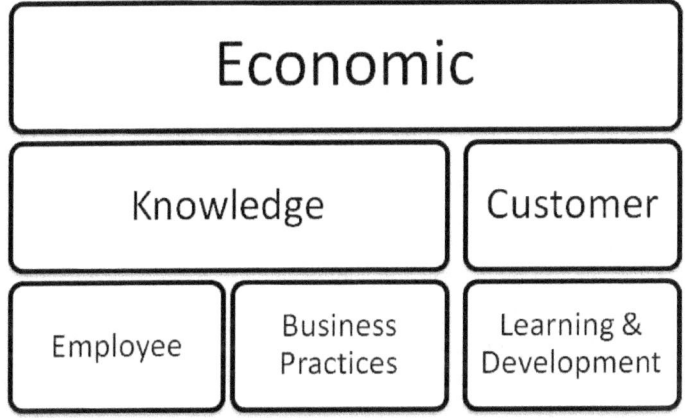

**Figure 1 – OKQ Measurement Framework**

## 1. Economic Context

Most of the modern day organizations are driven by the need to garner increased revenue while capping their expenses to the bare minimum. In order to optimize its revenue earning potential while providing a measure of autonomy, organizations are structured around key verticals or Small Business Units (SBU). The financial perspective should therefore include measures that are customized to suit the  individual requirements of these SBU's. However valuation techniques are scaled to an organizational level.

Financial objectives can differ considerably at each stage of an organization's life cycle. These stages can be broadly classified as follows:

1. The Sowing Stage
2. The Nurturing Stage
3. The Reaping Stage

The sowing stage represents the early stages of an organization's life cycle. The organization would have products or services with significant growth potential. To capitalize on this potential the organizational would have to commit considerable resources to develop and enhance its brand, construct and expand production facilities and nurture and develop customer relationships. Businesses in this stage would operate with negative cash flows and low current ROI.

It is every evident that during this stage the business would need to monitor its cash flows religiously. At this stage the cash flow techniques that can be employed include:

    *a.  Free Cash flows to Firm Approach*
    *b.  Price/Earnings (P/E) Multiples*

In the nurturing stage the organizational SBU's will be in a "sustain" mode where they would still need investment (CAPEX + OPEX), but would be expected to earn excellent returns on the capital employed. This stage mandates the requirement of financial objectives related to profitability and can be expressed by using measures related to accounting income. The following measures are recommended for this stage:

    *c.  Multiple Approach*
    *d.  Economic Value Added (EVA)*

The mature phase of an organization's life cycle is represented by the harvest stage or *Price/Sales (P/S)* the reaping stage wherein the organization expects to cash in on its efforts. In this stage the businesses no longer warrant significant investment – only enough to maintain equipment and capabilities (OPEX). The main goal is to maximize cash flow back to the organization. Thus financial objectives in this stage will emphasize traditional financial measurements like Return on Capital Employed (ROCE), operating income and gross margin. Investment projects in this category will be evaluated by discounted cash flow valuation techniques and capital budgeting analyses including:

    *a.  Discounted Cash flow*
    *b.  Dividend Discount Model*
    *c.  Free Cash flows to Equity (FCFE) Models*

## 2. Knowledge Context

The knowledge perspective includes the measures for organizations intangible assets, and is distinct from the financial perspectives presented in the preceding section. The key measure of organizational intangible assets is its Intellectual Capital (IC) or Knowledge Capital (KC).

Under the name of IC, we can classify all intangible resources (Bontis, 1996; Edvinsson and Malone, 1997; Roos and Roos, 1997), as well as their interconnections (Roos et al.,1997; Bontis, 1998). IC refers to the collection of intangible resources and their flows within the organization. Intangible assets contribute significantly to the bottom line of an organization, help maintain competitive advantage and build brand value that can be more than the physical valuation of the company itself. A case in point is web driven organizations like facebook, twitter flipkart and amazon. The goodwill earned by an enterprise is an intangible resource that contributes to the organizational IC pool. IC is specific to an organization – A top constituent of the IC pool of one organization may not be within the list of another. IC is therefore context specific. The value of an modern organization is a sum of its physical and monetary assets (financial capital), and collection of intangible resources. The figure 2 summarizes the above discussion.

Human capital is the collection of intangible resources that are embedded in the members of the organization. These resources can be of three main types:

a. **Competencies** (including skills and know-how)

b. **Attitude** (motivation, leadership qualities of the top management)

c. **Intellectual Agility** (the ability of members to adapt to changing organizational landscape)

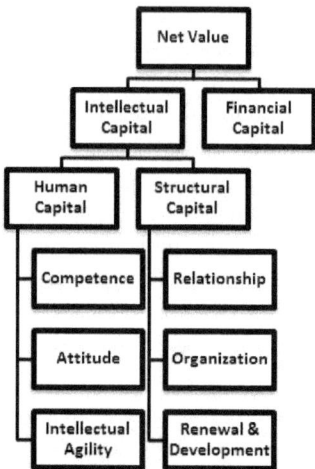

**Figure 2 - Organizational Value Chain**

According to a definition by Leif Edvinsson, Vice President and Corporate Director of IC for  field on KM), Structural capital is "everything that remains in the company after 5 o'clock",. The essence of structural capital is the knowledge embedded within the confines of an organization. Structural capital can be divided into relationships (suppliers, customers, allies, local communities, government, shareholders, etc.), organization (including structure, culture, routines and processes) and renewal and development (future projects, R&D, new initiatives etc.). It is essential, from an organizational perspective, to classify and identify the different types of IC and their flows. This is easier said than done since reporting of organizational IC flows is complex. IC flows do not necessarily add up to zero: in other words, IC management is not necessarily a zero-sum game (Roos and Roos, 1997). In fact, research has shown that knowledge and information are governed by increasing returns, as opposed to the decreasing returns, which characterize the traditional resources (land, labor and capital) (Arthur, 1996).

The choice of IC indicators should be guided by the long-term strategy of the organization- its vision or mission. Having established key differentiators and long term goals an organization should use these goals to identify two sets of variables: one is the "*value creating path*", that concentrates on IC that really drive value creation; the other is the set of *"key success factors"* (KSF) and indicators that track performance. The knowledge gleaned from these two separate streams should be converged to create a self-renewable IC framework illustrated in the figure 3:

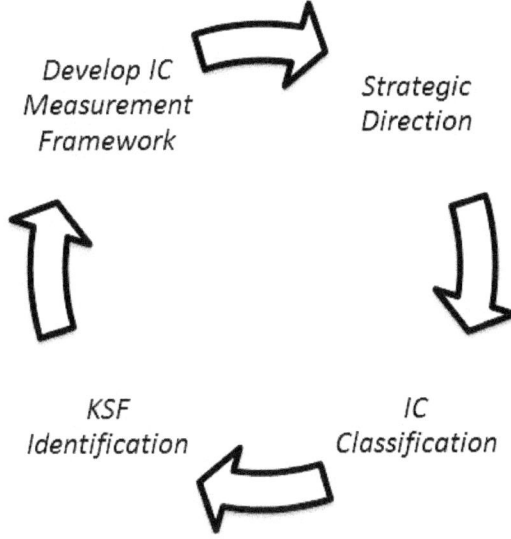

**Figure 3 - Organizational Intellectual Capital System**

The creation of an IC measurement system is fundamentally a top-down process. The initial framework has to be frozen with inputs from the top managements while the operational details have to be provided by the field employees. KSF are quite general, and in most cases refer to most organizations. The choice of indicators instead reflects the characteristics of the company more closely: in other words, it is more specific (Hauser and Katz, 1998). The challenge lies in the consolidation of the different IC indicators into a single, summary measure. The consolidated value is referred to as an IC index. The determination of the weightages of the constituents is most challenging part of developing the IC index. It may be noted there are no standards for developing an IC index, hence the constituents, weightages of the index would be different across organizations. Thus one cannot compare the absolute values if the index between organizations. However the changes in the index can be compared across organizations. Changes in this measure would reflect changes in the underlying components, which in turn would be a sign of changes at the deeper level of the drivers of future earning potential. Thus, a company that improved its IC index by 40% is invariably doing better than another that improved the same measure "only" by 30%.

## 3. Employee Context

The framework places the organizational members or knowledge workers in a separate perspective, since they form the core of organizations intellectual or intangible assets. Human capital represents the combined intelligence, skills and expertise that gives the organization its distinctive character. The human elements of the organization are those that are capable of learning, changing, innovating and providing the creative thrust which if properly motivated can ensure the long run survival of the organization.

Human Resource Accounting (HRA) is relevant to the valuation of intellectual assets in the new economy. According to Sackmann, Flamholtz and Bullen (1989, p. 235) the objective of HRA is to "quantify the economic value of people to the organization" in order to provide input for managerial and financial decisions. There are three types of HRA measurement models that are generally used:

a. *Cost Models* – Deals with the historical, acquisition, replacement or opportunity cost of human assets

b. *Human Resource (HR) Value Models* - which combine non-monetary behavioral with monetary economic value models

c. *Monetary Emphasis Models* - Determine discounted estimates of future earnings.

Measurement systems based on HRA have been used by service organizations including accounting firms, banks, insurance companies and financial services firms) where human capital comprises a significant proportion of organizational value. In their simplest form, HRA models attempt to calculate the contribution that human assets make to firms by capitalizing salary expenditures. In other words, instead of typically classifying total wages as an expense on the income statement, a discounted cash flow of total wages is classified in the asset section of the balance sheet.

## Example 1

*Assume an organization has one thousand employees whose average annual salary is one thousand units per employee.*

The traditional income statement method of expensing wages would yield a one million-currency unit expense (1,000 x 1,000) for the whole fiscal year. Using the HRA method requires a few more assumptions. First, HR managers would estimate the average length of tenure per employee as well as the average increase in wages per year. Therefore, the HRA measurement would consist of the one thousand employees; multiplied by the one thousand unit average salary; multiplied by the average length of tenure per employee; multiplied by the average increase in wages per year; all discounted back to year one. The residual figure is indicative of the human capital value of the firm.

One of the problems in using HRA is the difficulty in projecting the future size of an organization in the years to come. Furthermore, assumptions about tenure per employee, turnover and salary increases are all educated guesses. However HRA provides valuable internal feedback to organizational members on the accomplishment of strategic goals. It also serves as a launch pad to develop future plans and strategy by recognizing the core competencies inherent in the unique IC resident in the organization.

There are five employee outcome measurements recommended are listed below. The figure 4 illustrates the inter-relationship between these measures.

1. Employee Satisfaction
2. Employee Retention
3. Employee Productivity
4. Employee Competence
5. Employee Turnover

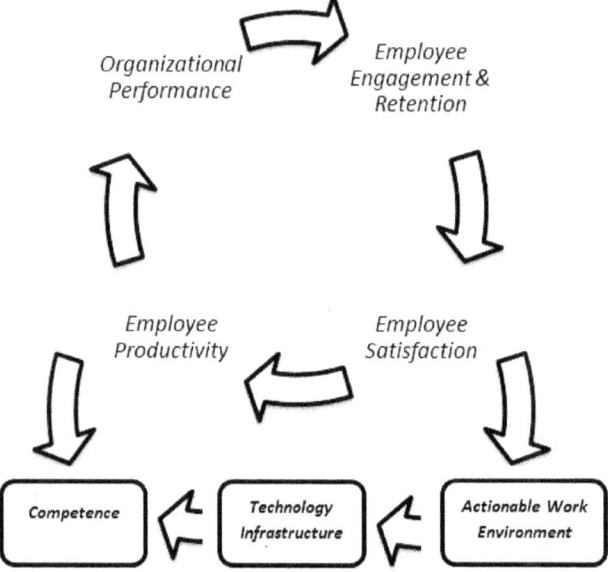

**Figure 4 – Measuring Employee Performance**

## *Measuring Employee Satisfaction*

This parameter can be measured with a survey for a specified percentage of randomly chosen employees. The use of technology as an enabler facilitates the online survey of all the employees. This will eliminate bias and provide accurate results. The survey can include questions based on key areas defining employee engagement and consequently employee satisfaction: These include the following:

a. Awareness of the strategic direction or long term focus of the organization
b. Involvement with decisions
c. Recognition for exceptional work
d. Resource availability for executing routine work
e. Support level from staff functions
f. Feedback on Compensation & Benefits structure
g. Feedback on Reward & Recognition structure
h. Career Planning & Succession Management
i. Overall satisfaction with the organization

### Measuring Employee Retention
This parameter is generally measured by percentage of key staff turnover

### Measuring Employee Productivity
This is an outcome measure of the aggregate impact from enhancing employee skills and morale, innovation, improving internal processes and customer satisfaction. The simplest productivity measure is revenue/employee.

### Measuring Employee Competence
The index for measuring employee competence (EC) has been based on statistical analysis of secondary data including data collected by Economic & Social Research Survey for its Works Centrality and Careers Project – WERS98 and BHPS (British Household Panel Survey) BHPS and supplemented by interviews using restricted judgmental sampling . The tables 2 – 8 lists the key parameters and their associated values for determining Employee Competence (Figure 5).

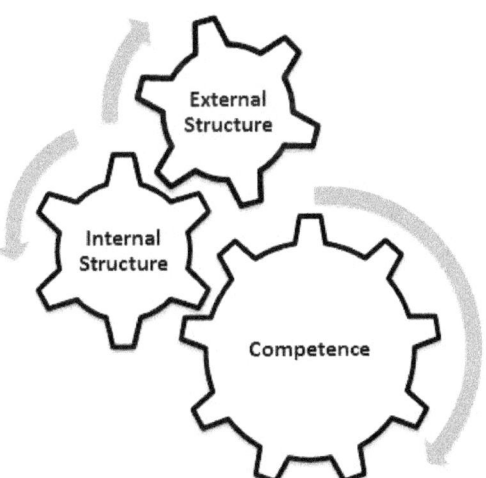

**Figure 5 - Employee Competence**

## Table 2 – Measuring Employee Competence

| Employee Competence Index (ECI) | | |
|---|---|---|
| S.N | Parameter | Weightage (%) |
| 1 | Academic Profile (x1) | 30 |
| 2 | Work Experience (x2) | 20 |
| 3 | Nature of Responsibility (x3) | 10 |
| 4 | Degree of Authority (x4) | 10 |
| 5 | Current Performance Rating(x5) | 10 |
| 6 | Contribution to Organization Knowledge Base (x6) | 20 |

## Table 3 – Academic Profile Computation

| Academic Proficiency Value (APV) | | |
|---|---|---|
| S.N | Parameter | Value |
| 1 | Primary | 0.1 |
| 2 | Secondary | 0.2 |
| 3 | High School | 0.3 |
| 4 | Graduation | 0.4 |
| 5 | Post-Graduation | 0.6 |
| 6 | Pre-Doctoral | 0.8 |
| 7 | Doctoral/Post-Doctoral | 1.0 |

## Table 4 – Work Experience Value Computation

| Employment Value (EV) | | |
|---|---|---|
| S.N | Parameter | Value |
| 1 | Exactly Same Profile (85-100%) | 1 |
| 2 | Mostly Matching Profile (55 -85%) | 0.75 |
| 3 | Partially Matching Profile (35-55%) | 0.4 |
| 4 | Different Profile (0-35%) | 0 |

Table 5 – Responsibility Value Computation

| Responsibility Span Value (RSV) | | |
| --- | --- | --- |
| S.N | Parameter | Value |
| 1 | Support Staff | 0.2 |
| 2 | Executive Level | 0.4 |
| 3 | Junior Management Cadre | 0.6 |
| 4 | Middle Management Cadre | 0.8 |
| 5 | Senior Management Cadre | 0.9 |
| 6 | Top Management Cadre | 1 |

Table 6 – Authority Value Computation

| Decision Making Value (DMV) | | |
| --- | --- | --- |
| S.N | Parameter | Value |
| 1 | Support | 0.5 |
| 2 | Operational / Field | 0.7 |
| 3 | Decision Making | 1 |

Table 7 – Current Performance (KRA)

| Performance Index (PI) | | |
| --- | --- | --- |
| S.N | Parameter (%) | Value |
| 1 | 90 -100 | 1 |
| 2 | 75 - 90 | 0.75 |
| 3 | 55 - 75 | 0.5 |
| 4 | 35 - 55 | 0.2 |
| 5 | 0 - 35 | 0 |

Table 8 – Contribution to Knowledge Base

| Intellectual Property Development (IPD) | | |
| --- | --- | --- |
| S.N | Parameter (%) | Value |
| 1 | Patents | 0.9 - 1.0 |
| 2 | Books Authored | 0.8 - 0.9 |
| 3 | Journal/ Conference Presentations | 0.7 |
| 4 | Copyrights/ Trademarks/ Other IPR | 0.6 |

| 5 | *Knowledge Generation/Conversion* | *0.1 – 0.5* |

*Employee Competence (EC)*
$$= (0.3 * x1 + 0.2 * x2 + 0.1 * x3 + 0.1 * x4 + 0.1 * x5 + 0.2 * x6)$$

*The value of EC will range between 0.12 and 1.0. The above matrix can be tweaked or customized depending upon specific organizational needs. A restricted judgmental sample could be employed for validation of the modified metrics. It may be noted that there are several other metrics for measuring competence at an organizational and individual level. It is however important to note that the metrics must be used consistently throughout the organizations (only one to be used, not multiple). These metrics serve as a reference for an organization to measure its competence/competency development.*

## 4. Customer Context

The customer perspective organizes measures relating to the identification of target groups for the products and services offered by an organization in addition to market-focused measures of customer satisfaction, retention, etc. This necessitates the identification of the primary customer and market segments along with the measures of the unit's performance in these targeted segments. This perspective typically includes several core or generic measures of the successful outcomes from a well formulated and implemented strategy. The core outcome measures (figure 3.6) include:

    a. Customer Satisfaction
    b. Customer Retention
    c. New Customer Acquisition
    d. Customer Profitability
    e. Market & Account Shares

It may be noted that each of the above measures have different implications for an organization and may relate to the performance of different verticals.

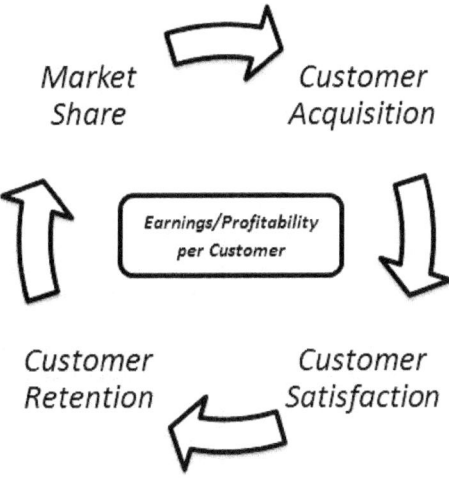

**Figure 6 - Customer Perspective – Core Measures**

### 5. Business Practices Context

This perspective identifies the processes that are the most critical for achieving customer and shareholder objectives. It is recommended that organizations outline their business practices and processes after formulating the objectives and measures for the financial, knowledge, employee and the customer perspectives. This sequence enables an organization to focus their internal-business process metrics on those processes that will fulfill the established objectives for customers and shareholders. The value chain is as depicted in the figure 7.

A useful metric that was developed for the manufacturing industry, but can be used in the service industry also, is Manufacturing Cycle Effectiveness (MCE). This metric was designed for the new age manufacturing units based on the For just-in-time (JIT) production flow. This unit can be customized to capture effectiveness of any project, product development including software and just about any product or service.

$$Manufacturing\ Cycle\ Effectiveness\ (MCE)$$
$$= \frac{Processing\ Time}{Throughput\ Time}$$

*Throughput Time = (Processing Time + Inspection Time + Movement Time + Waiting/Storage Time)*

It may be noted the ratio will be less than 1.

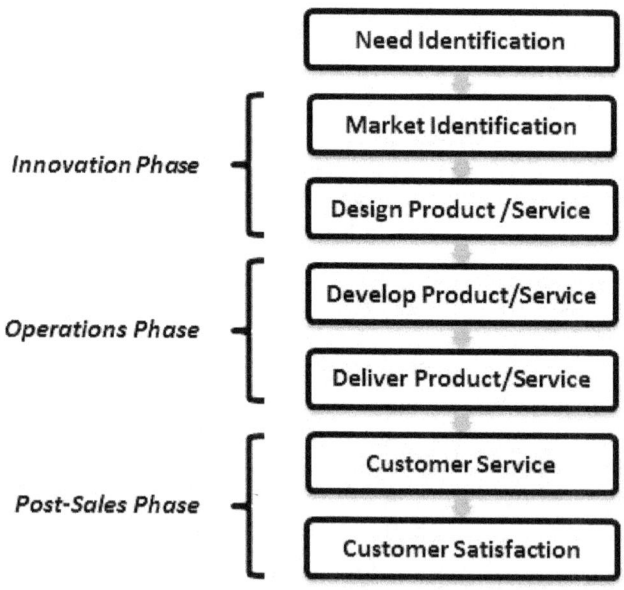

**Figure 7 - Organizational Internal Process Value Chain**

### 6. Learning & Development Context

This perspective includes all measures relating to employees and systems the company has in place to facilitate learning and knowledge dissemination. This perspective is extremely important in a learning organization since it develops objectives and measures to drive organizational learning and growth. The earlier perspectives identify the areas where an organization must excel to achieve breakthrough performance. The challenge lies in identifying situation specific unique drivers that spur organizational learning. This is as depicted in the table 3.9 below:

## Table 9 – Organizational Learning & Growth Drivers

| Employee Competence | Technology Framework | Actionable Work Environment |
|---|---|---|
| Strategic Skills | Strategic Technologies | Strategic Direction |
| | Knowledgebase | Decision Cycle Time |
| Knowledge Levels | Knowledge Conversion (Tacit to Explicit) | Employee Empowerment |
| | Patents, Copyrights, Trademarks and | Employee Engagement |
| Skill Leverage | other Intellectual Assets | Team Building |
| | | Employee Morale |

### Measures of Team Performance

It is a widely recognized fact that internal business process excellence cannot be achieved just by brilliant individual performances, but by a concerted team effort. This is especially true in case of service organizations for e.g. Project Teams in a software development industry. The five measures of team building and team performance that can be adopted by organizations are:

a. *Team Cohesion* – The metric could be represented as an absolute value or as a percentage and is generally crystallized through a survey. It represents the level of support and opportunity sharing between divisions, departments, SBU's, projects, teams or in general the different groups within an organization. Higher the value the greater would be the impact on EVA.

b. *Team Collaboration* – This metric, again represented as a value or in terms of percentages provides an indication of the degree of relationship between various groups within the organization. The value can be gleaned through the analysis of the work done or projects handled by common teams during a specified period.

c. *Integrated Engagements* – This value indicates the number of Projects with more than one division, department, SBU, group, team participation. This value is dependent the previous two parameters.

d. **Entrepreneurship** – This metric represents the number of teams developing their own business plan and/or other allied opportunities within the strategic framework of the organization.

e. *Distributed Reward & Recognition Structure* – There is no dispute to the fact that rewards and recognition, monetary in a large number of cases, spur individual and team performance. The presence of a robust reward & recognition (R&R) structure can have a significant impact on employee productivity. In industries that require higher levels of team participation as opposed to individual participation the, R&R should be tailored to facilitate incentive sharing by team members based on their contribution and performance towards common goals. The three measures that could be employed for measurement of team based R&R structure are:
   i. Percentage of projects with shared R&R
   ii. Percentage of projects with potential shared R&R
   iii. Percentage of projects with individual/team specific incentives linked to project achievements

One of the most critical factors in measuring and managing organizations intellectual assets is the success or effectiveness of its knowledge sharing efforts. Knowledge acquisition and dissemination can be through formalized interventions like Instructor Lead Training (ILT), On-the-Job-Training, e-learning, Web based learning or other similar interventions. A 'Collaborative Blended Virtual Learning Environment' (CBVLE) which integrates the advantaged of all the methodologies listed above is recommended for organizations with a large geographic spread. Irrespective of the intervention chosen, the two important aspects to be determined are the effectiveness of the trainer and the satisfaction levels of the participants. Accordingly the following metrics can be used to measure the effectiveness of an organizations knowledge sharing efforts:
   i. *Training Delivery Index (TDI)*
   ii. *Trainee Satisfaction Index (TSI)*
These measures have been arrived at by analyzing a structured questionnaire (Table 10) distributed to participants, of varying knowledge levels, academic profile, technical background, work

experience and cadres over a wide range of training programs.

**Table 10 - Parameters for determining TDI/TSI**

| S.N | Parameter | Rating |
|---|---|---|
| 1 | Course Coverage (x1) | |
| 2 | Communication Skills (x2) | |
| 3 | Presentation Skills (x3) | |
| 4 | Query Handling Ability (x4) | |
| 5 | Participant Involvement (x5) | |
| 6 | Class Room/Lab Setup (x6) | |
| 7 | Job Relevance (x7) | |
| 8 | Course Design & Structure (x8) | |
| 9 | Courseware Quality (x9) | |
| 10 | Effectiveness of Training Program (x10) | |
| 11 | Course Administration (x11) | |

The rating system for the above parameters is presented in table 11:

**Table 11- Rating Scale for Training Effectiveness**

| Rating | Value |
|---|---|
| 6 | Excellent |
| 5 | Very Good |
| 4 | Good |
| 3 | Satisfactory |
| 2 | Average |
| 1 | Poor |

$Training\ Delivery\ Index\ (TDI)$

$$= \left\{ \left[ 0.75 * \left( \frac{\sum_{i=1}^{n}(x1 + x2 + x3)_i}{n} \right) / 6 * 100 \right] + \left[ 0.25 * \left( \frac{\sum_{i=1}^{n}(x4 + x5)_i}{n} \right) / 6 * 100 \right] \right\}$$

TDI is expressed as a percentage. x1..n represents the average rating for the specified parameter for the entire batch.

*Trainee Satisfaction Index (TSI)*

$$= \left\{ \left[ 0.5 * \frac{\left( \frac{\sum_{i=1}^{n}(x2 + x3 + x4 + x5)_i}{n} \right)}{6} * 100 \right] \right.$$

$$+ \left[ 0.3 * \frac{\left( \frac{\sum_{i=1}^{n}(x6 + x7 + x8 + x9 + x10)_i}{n} \right)}{6} \right.$$

$$\left. * 100 \right] + 0.2 * \left[ \left( \frac{\sum_{i=1}^{n}\left(\frac{x2}{n}\right)_i}{6} \right) * 100 \right] \right\}$$

TDI is expressed as a percentage. x1..n represents the average rating for the specified parameter for the entire batch.

The above equations have been expressed in a simplified fashion so as to make the significance apparent to the reader.

The figure 8 sums up the key metrics presented in the framework:

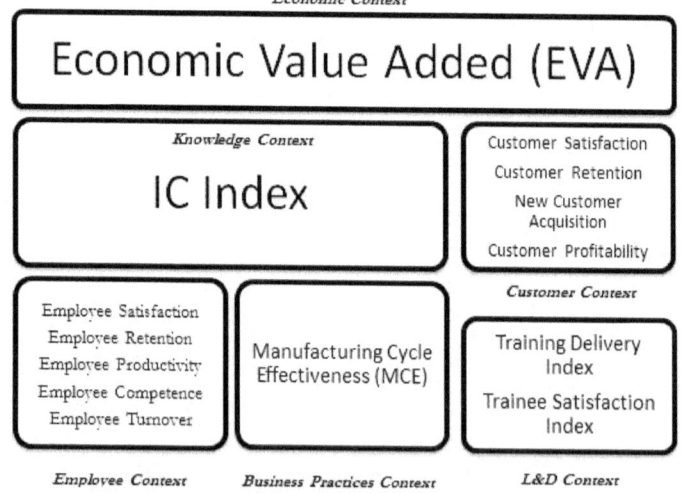

**Figure 8 – IC Measurement Framework – Key Metrics**

# 4 DEPLOYING OKQ FRAMEWORK

The theoretical constructs presented in the above sections can be fully appreciated only if the deployment aspects are well understood by the reader. This can be achieved through a concrete example that provides a linkage between the different elements of the framework. It must be noted that the measures provides as a part of the framework are for indicative purpose only. Depending upon the nature of industry and specific requirements, some of these measures may not be relevant, while some of the others may need to be customized. The objective was to provide a concrete methodology for building and evaluating organizational competence.

**Example 2**

Focal Training is a learning solutions provider based out of Seattle – US, which commenced its operations in 2011, by providing classroom based or instructor-led-training (ILT) by providing learning services to corporate as well as retail clientele. By early 2012 it realized, though its operations had grown to a modest $50,000, the brick-and-mortar operations was quite capital intensive and also limited its portfolio. It soon started to offer its services over the web using a simple e-learning platform. The platform was used to supplement its ILT operations, reduce cycle times, and enhance resource utilization. The growth rate through 2012 and early 2013 was flat even though the operations had settled. Focal tried to boost its revenues by beefing up its marketing and sales operations. It could increase its market share, however the backend operations could not scale up to the increased number of participants. Customer satisfaction levels started falling and the company's topline was taking a hit. The company wanted to expand its footprint to the entire US and internationally to Canada, Australia, New Zealand and India. The efforts were stymied since the management team was not experienced in understanding the complexities of supporting such a large operation. It roped in a specialist who was well versed with setting up and running large learning organizations as well as managing and harnessing organizational intellectual capital effectively.

A cursory examination of the organization revealed that there were multiple problems that were hampering the organizations growth. The overall mission/vision of the company was smudged, there was no evidence of any strategic leadership and direction, product lines were not clear, product quality was suspect, internal process and procedures were not documented, customer feedback was not solicited and used for process improvement.

The L&D industry is technology intensive and the customer satisfaction is directly linked to the trainer – direct or virtual. The supporting environment also does have an impact on trainee satisfaction. The subsequent section provides a detailed treatise on implementing the OKQ framework.

The process commenced with the set-up of a management team which began with a relook at its mission/vision statement. After hectic discussions it was felt that the previous vision was not commensurate with the management expectations, not documented and represented a set of abstract thoughts by the top management. Accordingly the reworked statements was articulated as follows:

**Vision:** *"Empower individuals achieve career and professional aspirations"*

**Mission:** *"Provide World-Class, Competency based, On-Demand Learning Solutions"*

This translated into three key pivotal areas for the company. These included:

1. Dynamic Product Development
2. Optimal Process Management

3. Optimized Business Practices

The focus was to be on a limited number of products (three) in tune with the existing near term demands, potential for upgrade in the long-term. The business processes (internal) would be synchronized to meet this demand – This includes the entire academic lifecycle including development-delivery-evaluation-feedback-innovation. The emphasis was on the use and leverage of cutting-edge technology including deployment of Learning Management System (LMS) with integrated assignment grading and assessment engine, instructional design and course evaluation and feedback interfaces and the setup of a Virtual Collaborative Blended Learning Environment (VCBLE). The broad framework is illustrated in figure 9.

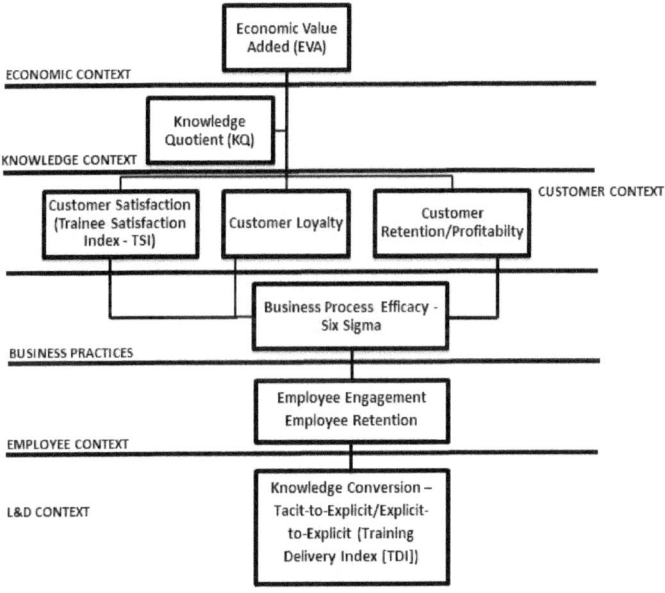

**Figure 9 – Example of OKQ Framework Deployment**

The above example, though real, is for indicative process only. The design and deployment of an organizational competence measurement framework is complex and beyond the immediate scope of this work. The example 3.2 presented a simplified application of the OKQ framework.

# 5 FINANCIAL VALUATION TECHNIQUES

## Discounted Cash Flow

Discounted cash flow (DCF) is a method of valuing an organization by estimating the time value of money. The future cash flows of an organization are estimated and discounted to give their present values. This sum, of all future (receipts as well as expenses), is defined as the net present value (NPV). Exponential discounting is the commonly used method of discounting. NPV is estimated as the amount to be invested currently at a specified rate of return in order to obtain the future cash flows.

$$\text{Discounted Cash Flow (DCF)} = \frac{CF_1}{(1+r)^1} + \frac{CF_2}{(1+r)^2} + \dots \frac{CF_n}{(1+r)^n}$$

Where 'CF' represents the cash flows, 'n' the number of years and 'r' indicates the interest/discount rate (cost of tying up capital along with the associated risks).

Accordingly:

$$Future\ Value\ (FV) = DCF * (1 + r)^n$$

and

$$Discounted\ Present\ Value\ (DPV) = \frac{FV}{(1+r)^n}$$

The above equation is for organizations with only cash flow in a given time period. Normally organizations would have multiple cash flows spread over multiple time periods. In such cases:

$$DPV = \sum_{t=0}^{n} \frac{FV_t}{(1+r)^t}$$

### Dividend Discount Model

Dividend Discount Model (DDM) is a method of valuating the stocks of an organization based on the NPV of the future dividends. It is expressed by the equation:

$$Current\ Stock\ Price\ (P) = \frac{D_1}{(r-g)}$$

### Economic Value Added (EVA)

The traditional financial measures of performance, like Return on Assets (ROA) and Return on Equity (ROE) have several shortcomings and are losing relevance in the modern business environment. A primary drawback is that they do not consider the cost of capital incurred to fund the projects. They are also highly aggregated due to which the impact of different strategic factors cannot be clearly separated and understood (Stewart, 1994). In addition they often fail to shed light on underlying causes of high or low performance.

Stern Stewart & Co., a New York-based consulting firm, introduced economic Value Added (EVA) in the late 1980s as a tool to assist corporations to pursue their prime financial directive by aiding in maximizing the wealth of their shareholders (Stewart,

35

1994). In the broadest terms, EVA is a comprehensive financial management measurement system that can be used to tie together capital budgeting, financial planning, goal setting, performance measurement, and shareholder communication in addition to incentive compensation. The objective of EVA is to develop a performance measure that properly accounts for all ways in which corporate value could be added or lost.

Building accountability into a measurement system, EVA encourages managers to take each and every decision following the overarching principle of maximizing shareholder value. Thus EVA is the only measure of performance that properly accounts for all the complex trade-offs involved in creating value.

EVA provides a common language and benchmark for managers to discuss value creation: projects become easily comparable, and managers can respond to the pressure for performance accountability through the use of an appropriate metrics (Young, 1998).

The difference in the capital invested in an organization and the market capitalization is referred to as market value added (MVA). The spread represents the difference between the capital infused by the organizational shareholders, since inception, and the value gained by selling the shares at its present value. The greater the spread, greater would be the earnings of the shareholders (Bontis, Dragonetti, Jacobsen & Roos, 1999). The MVA represents net present value (NPV) of current and proposed capital investment projects as perceived by the markets . MVA is thus a significant summary assessment of corporate performance - showing how successful a company has been in allocating, managing and redeploying scarce resources to maximize the NPV of the enterprise and hence the wealth of the shareholders.

EVA is defined by the following equation:

CAPEX is calculated as the weighted average of the cost of capital multiplied by the total capital. Hence EVA increases if the weighted average cost of capital is less than the return on net assets, and vice versa.

Even though EVA does not explicitly relate to the management of intangible resources the effective management of knowledge assets will increase EVA. EVA can be considered as a surrogate measure for the stock of IC and that EVA can be viewed as a measure for return on IC (Marchant and Barsky, 1997). The implication is that these investments should still be judged according to the standard criteria for assessing any long-term project: net present value, cost benefit analysis, etc. In defining the EVA measures, Stern Stewart & Co. has identified 164 different areas of performance adjustments that are supposed to address shortcomings in conventional accounting practice, and thus solve problems like the accounting of intangibles and long-term investments with a high degree of uncertainty. These include depreciation, capitalization and amortization of R&D, market building, outlays, restructuring charges, acquisition premiums and other "strategic" investments with deferred pay off patterns.

## Free Cash flows to Equity Model

Free Cash Flows to Equity (FCFE) represents the amount of cash dividend that can be made to the equity shareholders of an organization after deducting all expenses, making provisions for reinvestment and debt repayments. In simple terms FCFE can be represented as:

$$FCFE = Net\ Income$$
$$- CAPEX_{net} - Working\ Captial_{net}Changes$$
$$+ Debt_{new} - Debt_{repayment}$$

### Free Cash Flows to Firm

Free Cash Flows to Firm (FCFF) refers to the surplus cash generated by an organization after meeting all its requirements and commitments. This surplus cash can be distributed amongst the debt and equity holders of the organization. In simple terms FCFF can be expressed as:

$$FCFF = Cash\ Flow_{Investments} + Cash\ Flow_{Operations}$$

A more common approach of computing FCFF is:

$$FCFF = EBIT * (1 - t_r) + Expenditures_{Non\ Cash}$$
$$+ Working\ Capital_{Changes} - CAPEX$$

## Multiple Approach

Multiple Approach refers to a valuation theory based on the premise that the value of comparable assets would mostly be similar. This approach is based on the comparison of the value of an organization based on that of another comparable organization. The comparison is based on ratios of key organizational performance indicators including operating margins and cash flows.

## Price/Earnings Multiples

The Price/Earnings (P/E) Multiples is an equity valuation ratio that is defined as the ratio of the market price of a share (equity) of an organization to the annual earnings per share. This measure provides a means of analyzing the market valuation of an organization and its equity relative to the income generated by it from its operations. This measure is generally used for peer evaluation of organizations.

# SUMMARY

Intellectual Capital remains the most unexploited resource within an organization. Knowledge continues to be seen as a static organizational asset. This is especially true for organizations in the Indian subcontinent. The tremendous growth in the different fields of management and research contributions in the last decade have not helped in addressing all the limitations in measurement models. The framework presented in this chapter builds on the advantages and the robustness of the Balanced Score Card while doing away with some of its primary limitations, namely rigidity, traditional financial measures, lack of employee perspective etc. The deployment of IC, EVA and HRA within the modified six dimensional framework is unique and provides a more holistic measurement framework.

The framework presented in this chapter is more than just a collection of measures. It is imperative that all measures should be allied through a causative chain that terminates with a linkage to monetary performance. The effectiveness of the strategic direction of an organization should be monitored continually to get a feedback on its framework. The organization should effect single measure changes and check its effects till it manages to fine-tune all the metrics in the framework. This is a continual process wherein the cause-and-effect relationships are modified cyclically.

| Measuring Organizational Competence | Organizational Intellectual Capital |
|---|---|
| | Valuating Intellectual Capital |
| | Understanding the measurement framework |

# USEFUL LINKS

http://www.business.mcmaster.ca/mktg/nbontis/ic/publications/
BontisEMJ.pdf
http://www.willamette.com/insights_journal/12/autumn_2012_2.
pdf
http://en.wikipedia.org/wiki/Intellectual_capital
http://www.opf.slu.cz/vvr/akce/turecko/pdf/Akpinar.pdf
http://www.orgmasz.pl/wydawnictwo/files/Intellectual.pdf

# KEY TERMS

Accounting For The Future (AFTF)
Balanced Scorecard (BSC)
British Household Panel Survey (BHPS)
Capital Expenditure (CAPEX)
Collaborative Blended Virtual Learning Environment (CBVLE)
Direct Intellectual Capital Methods (DICM)
Economic Value Added (EVA)
Employee Competence (EC)
Free Cash Flows To Equity (FCFE)
Human Resource Accounting (HRA)
Human Resource Costing & Accounting (HRCA)
Human Resources (HR)
Instructor Lead Training (ILT)
Intangible Asset Monitor (IAM)
Intellectual Asset Valuation (IAV)
Intellectual Capital (IC)
Intellectual Capital (IC)
Intellectual Capital Navigator And Intellectual Capital Index (IC Index)
Investor Assigned Market Value (IAMV)
Just-In-Time (JIT)
Key Success Factors (KSF)
Knowledge Management (KM)
Manufacturing Cycle Effectiveness (MCE)
Market Capitalization Methods (MCM)
Market Value Added (MVA
Net Present Value (NPV)
Operational Expenditure (OPEX)
Research & Development (R&D)
Return On Assets (ROA)
Return On Capital Employed (ROCE
Return-On-Investment (ROI)
Reward & Recognition (R&R)
Scorecard Methods (SC)
Small Business Units (SBU)
Total Value Creation (TVC)
Trainee Satisfaction Index (TSI)
Training Delivery Index (TDI)

Value Added Intellectual Coefficient (VAIC)
Works Centrality And Careers Project (WERS)

# REFERENCES

Bontis, Nick. (1996). "There's a Price on your Head: Managing Intellectual Capital Strategically", *Business Quarterly*, Summer, 40-47.

Bontis, Nick. (1998). "Intellectual Capital: An exploratory study that develops measures and models", *Management Decision*, 36, 2, 63-76.

Edvinsson, L., and M.S. Malone, 1997, *Intellectual Capital*, Piatkus, London.

Jurczak Jolanta (2008). *Intellectual Capital Measurement Methods*, Institute of Organization and Managment in Industry. ORGMASZ" Vol 1(1); p. 37 – 45, 10.2478/v10061-008-0005-y.

Luthy, D.H. (1998): *Intellectual capital and its measurement*. paper presented at the Asian Pacific Interdisciplinary Research in Accounting (APIRA) Conference, Osaka, available at: www3.bus.osaka-cu.ac.jp/apira98/archives/htmls/25.htm

Marchant, G. and Barsky, N.P. (1997) Invisible but valuable? A framework for the measurement and management of intangible assets. Paper presented at 2nd World Congress on the *Management of Intellectual Capital*, Hamilton, ON, 21–23 January.

Nick Bontis, Nicola C. Dragonetti, Kristine Jacobsen and Göran Roos (1999). *THE KNOWLEDGE TOOLBOX: A Review of the Tools Available To Measure and Manage Intangible Resources.*

Roos G., Pike S., Fernstrom L., *Managing Intellectual Capital in Practice*, Butterworth-Heinemann, New York 2005, p. 19.

Roos, G. and Roos, J. (1997) Measuring your company's intellectual performance. *Long Range Planning* 30(3), 413–426.

Roos, J., Roos, G., Dragonetti, N.C. and Edvinsson, L. (1997) *Intellectual Capital: Navigating in the New Business Landscape.* Macmillan, Houndmills, Basingtoke.

Sackmann, S., Flamholz, E. and Bullen, M. (1989) Human resource accounting: a state of the art review. *Journal of Accounting Literature* 8, 235–264.

Stewart III, G.B. (1994) EVA: fact and fantasy. *Journal of Applied Corporate Finance* 7(Summer), 71–84.

Young, S.D. (1998) Economic value added. INSEAD case, no. 4667.

# INDEX

## A

Accounting For The Future (AFTF) · 8
Attitude · 15

## B

Balanced Scorecard (BSC) · 6, 41
Benchmarking · 6, 9
Brand Equity Valuation – · 7
Business Process Auditing · 6
Business Worth · 6

## C

Calculated Intangible Value · 7, 8
Citation Weighted Patents · 8
Collaborative Blended Virtual Learning Environment' (CBVLE) · 28
Competence · 3, 12, 19, 21, 22, 27, 41
Competency Index · 8
Competency Models · 6
Competency Quotient · 8
Cost Models · 18

## D

Direct Intellectual Capital Methods (DICM) · 7
Discounted Cash Flow · 14
Distributed Reward & Recognition Structure · 28
Dividend Discount Model · 14, 35

## E

Economic Value Added (EVA) · 9, 14, 35, 41
Employee Competence · 19
Employee Productivity · 19, 21
Employee Retention · 19, 21
Employee Satisfaction · 19
Employee Turnover · 19
Entrepreneurship · 28

## F

Free Cash Flows To Equity (FCFE) Models · 14
Free Cash Flows To Firm Approach · 14

## H

Human Capital Intelligence ·

# ABOUT THE AUTHOR

Sudhir Warier is a Human Capability Management Coach with expertise in organizational knowledge management and a proven track record in developing and leading learning organizations. He has over 20years of experience with over 14 years in leading the Learning & Development and Human Capital Management function. He has hands-on experience in managing the entire organization Learning & Development and Human Capital Management value chain including training delivery (Corporate/Retail), academic management, curriculum development, R&D, Talent Management, Coaching and Mentoring. He has also spent over 15 years in the field of Knowledge Management (Intellectual Capital Management) engaged in research activities, developing organizational frameworks and assessing organizational competency management initiatives. He has authored seven books and published over 30 high quality research papers in international conferences and peer reviewed journals. His book titled 'Knowledge Management' is a best seller and a reference text for varied university degree and post graduate courses internationally.

## OTHER PUBLICATIONS

| S.N | Name | ISBN |
|-----|------|------|
| 1 | Knowledge Management | 978-8125913634 |
| 2 | Data Warehousing Essentials | 978-1463590482 |
| 3 | Data Mining Fundamentals | 978-1484145463 |
| 4 | Optical Communication Fundamentals | 978-1482615791 |
| 5 | Strategic Management | - |
| 6 | Management Theory & Practice | - |
| 7 | Competency Management – The Conceptual Framework | 978-1499236972 |
| 8 | A Framework for Measuring Intangible Assets | 978-1502869340 |
| 9 | Competency Quotient | 978-1502863454 |
| 10 | Competency Mapping & Management – A Comprehensive Survey Report | 978-1502870292 |